Milet Publishing
Smallfields Cottage, Cox Green
Rudgwick, Horsham, West Sussex
RH12 3DE England
info@milet.com
www.milet.com
www.milet.co.uk

First English–French edition published by Milet Publishing in 2013

Copyright © Milet Publishing, 2013

ISBN 978 1 84059 840 7

Original Turkish text written by Erdem Seçmen
Translated to English by Alvin Parmar and adapted by Milet

Illustrated by Chris Dittopoulos
Designed by Christangelos Seferiadis

Printed and bound in Turkey by Ertem Matbaası

My Bilingual Book

Touch
Le toucher

English–French

How do you know what's smooth or rough?

Comment sais-tu que quelque chose est lisse ou rugueux ?

Your hands are your sensors, they're sensitive and tough!

Tes mains sont des capteurs à la fois solides et sensibles !

If you play without gloves in the snow,

Si tu joues dans la neige sans gants,

your hands will get cold, you know!

tu sais que tu auras froid aux mains !

Teddy bear feels soft and furry.

L'ours en peluche est doux.

Play-dough feels nicely squishy!

La pâte à modeler est agréablement douce et humide !

Your skin is the part of you that understands

Ta peau est la partie de ton corps qui éprouve

how different things feel in your hands.

a sensation que te procurent les différentes choses entre tes mains.

The touch sense comes from nerves in your skin

Le sens du toucher provient des nerfs de ta peau,

that travel to your brain and say, message in!

qui envoient un message à ton cerveau !

Your brain decides quickly what to do

Ton cerveau décide rapidement de ce qu'il faut faire

and nerves send the message back to you!

et le message t'est renvoyé par les nerfs !

So when you touch something sharp,

Si tu touches quelque chose qui pique,

your nerves tell you, stop!

tes nerfs te disent d'arrêter !

Or they tell you to be gentle

Ils te disent d'être délicat

when you touch a soft petal.

quand tu touches les pétales d'une fleur.

Touch helps you learn about nature and things.

Le toucher permet de découvrir la nature et les objets.

It's really amazing, all the knowledge it brings!

C'est incroyable toutes les connaissances qu'il apporte !

Your touch can also show you care,

Le toucher permet également de montrer ton affection,

like hugging someone who is dear.

comme quand tu serres quelqu'un que tu aimes dans tes bras.